# PLANET EARTH

Design        Cooper · West

Editor        Margaret Fagan

Researcher    Cecilia Weston-Baker

Illustrator   Louise Nevett

Consultant    J. W. Warren Ph.D.
              Formerly Reader in Physics
              Education, Department of
              Physics, Brunel University,
              London, UK

Published by Price Stern Sloan, Inc.
360 North La Cienega Boulevard, Los Angeles, California 90048

# PLANET EARTH

## Mark Pettigrew

PRICE STERN SLOAN

Los Angeles

# INTRODUCTION

The planet Earth is our home. It is also home to millions of different plants and animals. Like the human race, the planet Earth has a history, only many millions of years longer.

In this book you will find out how the Earth began, what it is like today, and how it is changing. You will see how movements in the Earth's surface produce mountains, earthquakes and volcanoes. And you will see how the spinning Earth creates the pattern of night and day.

You will also discover how Earth's movement around the Sun causes the seasons and the tides.

# CONTENTS

# PLANET EARTH

When you stand on a beach and look out to sea, the horizon, or skyline, seems curved. This is because our Earth is shaped like a ball; it measures about 13,000km (8,000 miles) across. The land and water that you can see are only a small part of the surface of this ball.

Seen from space Earth is almost perfectly round and appears to have a smooth surface. The highest mountain on the land is 10km (6 miles) high, and the deepest ocean is about 11km (7 miles) deep. This is very small compared to the size of the Earth.

The Earth is one of many planets in our solar system. However, it is the only planet which has the right conditions for human life. Other planets would be too cold or too hot for us to live there, or the atmosphere would be too poisonous.

Our planet Earth is made up of oceans . . .

. . . the atmosphere

7

. . . and the land

# HOW THE EARTH BEGAN

The Earth began an astonishing 4.6 billion years ago. We believe that the Earth and the other planets were formed from a flat, rotating gas and dust cloud. This cloud formed into small, cold particles which attracted one another, collided, and formed larger particles. All this took place over millions of years. As the larger particles collided, they became hot and melted. Iron from these formed the central core of the Earth, and other substances surrounded it.

The molten outer layer of the Earth cooled to form a thin shell, and the inside was kept warm by violent reactions within. Sometimes molten rock escaped from beneath the Earth's surface in volcanic eruptions. Gases escaped from inside the early Earth to form an "atmosphere."

**Structure of the Earth**
The outer layer of the Earth is a thin, solid skin, called the "crust." Below it is a region called the "mantle." The outer layer of the mantle is made of molten rock, called "magma." Below the mantle is a region of molten rock under great pressure. The central region of the Earth is a solid core. The temperature in the core is probably about 6,000°C (10,800°F).

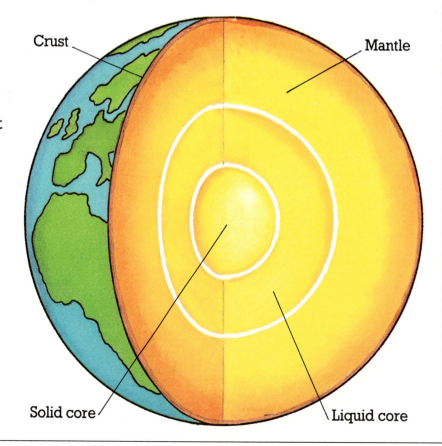

Crust

Mantle

Solid core

Liquid core

9

Volcanoes occur where the Earth's crust is weak and rock can escape

# CHANGING EARTH

The remains of ancient animals, or "fossils," tell us that our planet and the life on it were once very different from how they are today. Throughout the ages, the Earth and its climate have changed, sometimes very slowly – sometimes more rapidly. For example, the climate changed dramatically with the coming of the ice ages. The most recent ice age started about 70,000 years ago, and lasted about 60,000 years.

As the Earth changed, the plants and animals living on it also changed. Often this was a reaction to changes in the Earth, but sometimes the plants and animals caused changes in the Earth. For example, some garden soil was partly formed from the rotting remains of dead plants and animals, called "humus."

The fossil remains of a dinosaur – possibly 200 million years old

Imagine the changes of Earth's lifetime squashed to fit into a 24-hour day. On this scale, there would be no life on Earth until about 6:30 a.m., when the first microscopic plants and animals would appear. Large animals with backbones, like fish, would not appear until about 9:15 p.m. Reptiles would appear at about 10:30 p.m. Mammals would appear at about 11 p.m., but only become common about 11:40 p.m. People appear on Earth 40 seconds before midnight. All written history takes place in the last tenth of a second of a day.

# MOVING CONTINENTS

The Earth's crust is only very thin, and is formed of large, flat pieces, called "tectonic plates." Each plate may be thousands of miles across. These plates are moved very slowly by movements of the magma underneath. Where two plates push against each other, they rise up to form mountains. Where they move apart, oceans form, and magma can escape to form new rocks.

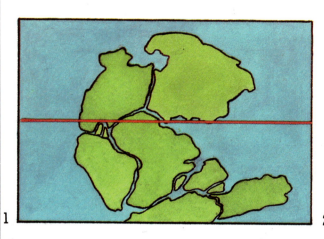

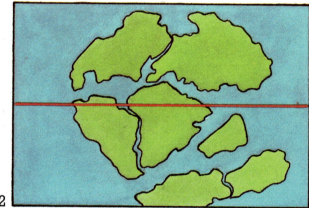

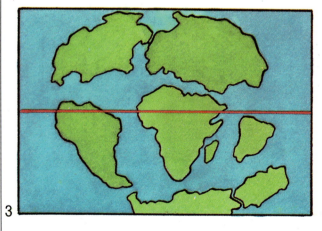

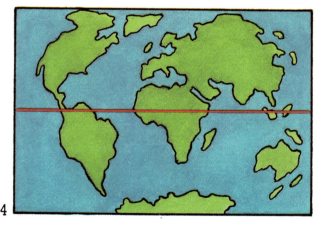

**200 to 135 million years ago**
The main land masses that we know today were all grouped close together (1). Over many millions of years, the continental plates moved away from one another (2).

**65 million years ago to today**
The continents began to look as they do today (3). The continents are still moving but nevertheless you can still see how they once could fit together (4). How will they appear in 100 million years time?

When tectonic plates press against each other, they do not slide smoothly. Instead, they press and press until suddenly they break at a weak point. As they break, there may be a sudden movement of the crust, which we feel as an earthquake.

Occasionally, some of the mantle can push through weak points in the crust and form a volcano. The crust is usually weaker along or near the lines where plates meet.

You see the effects of an earthquake as cracks in the Earth's surface

# ROCKS AND EROSION

Rocks are not really as permanent as they seem. Rain, wind and freezing weather all help to break them up into tiny pieces, which are washed away by rain and rivers. This process is called "erosion." Where rivers slow down or meet the sea, these tiny pieces of rock are left behind – they form a "sediment," such as sand or mud. The layers of sediment gradually thicken as more sand or mud is deposited, and the tiny pieces become stuck together under great pressure to form rocks. As these rocks are formed from sediments, they are called "sedimentary" rocks.

Erosion and sedimentation are slow processes. They may take thousands of years to have a noticeable effect on the landscape about us.

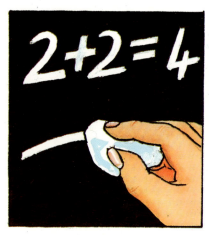

**Sedimentary rocks**
"Sedimentary" rocks are made of layers of small particles. For example, chalk cliffs are made from layers of very small shells and skeletons of sea animals.

**Metamorphic rocks**
Sedimentary rocks are changed when they are subjected to heat and pressure deep in the Earth's crust. This is how "metamorphic" rocks, like marble, are formed.

**Igneous rocks**
"Igneous" rocks are formed from magma which has cooled, either slowly inside the Earth, or quickly on the surface. Pumice and granite are formed in this way.

15

Rock formations caused by erosion in the Utah desert

# RICHES OF THE EARTH

All the metals we use are taken from the Earth. Most of them are found combined with other substances, in rocks called ores, and have to be extracted before they can be used. Some, like gold and copper, may be found as the pure metal.

Many of the fuels we use, like coal, gas and oil, are also taken from the Earth. These are called "fossil fuels." Coal is usually dug out of the ground. Gas and oil are obtained by drilling deep holes in the Earth and carrying the gas or oil through a pipe to where it is needed.

Rocks in the Earth's crust can often be used for specialized jobs. For example, one rock called "mica" is found in thin, transparent sheets. It can be used to make windows in high-temperature ovens, where glass would melt.

**How coal was formed**

Coal has formed over millions of years from the remains of ancient forests growing on swamps (1). As forest trees and plants died, they fell into the swamps forming layers of dead vegetation. Later, sedimentary rocks formed on top of these layers (2). The pressure caused by the rocks made the layers of vegetation denser and harder (3), and formed them into a solid rock – coal (4).

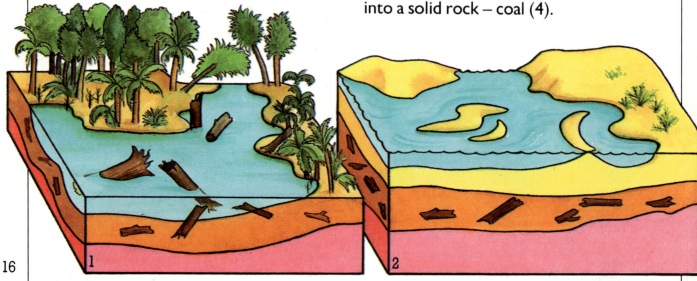

Coal is a fossil fuel often mined from underground

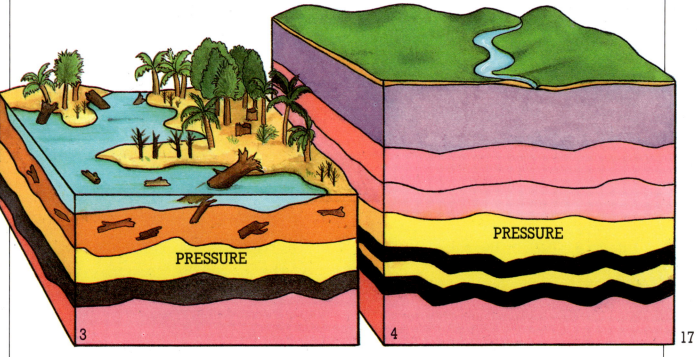

3

4

# EARTH'S OCEANS

The oceans cover about two-thirds of the Earth's surface and have existed for more than 3 billion years!

The top layer of the ocean has a rich plant and animal life, called "plankton." Millions of these tiny organisms produce food for all the other sea animals. Plankton is one of the oldest forms of life on Earth. Deeper down at about a hundred yards, it is too dark for plants to grow, so the ocean bottom is mostly bare.

Winds blowing across the ocean cause waves. When winds blow over a great distance across the sea, they build up waves which may be many feet tall.

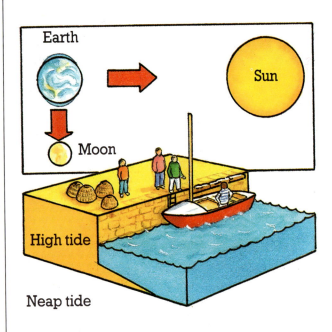

Neap tide

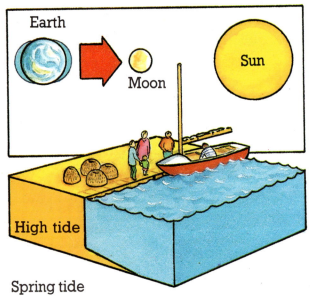

Spring tide

## The tides

Tides are caused by the pull of the Moon and the Sun on the waters of the Earth. When the Sun and Moon are out of line with the Earth, their pulls oppose each other, and the tides are not very high. These are called "neap tides." But when both the Sun and the Moon are in line with the Earth, their pulls add up, and the tides are very high. These are called "spring tides."

The oceans cover much of the Earth's surface

# SPINNING EARTH

The Sun appears to us as if it moves around the Earth. In fact, it is the Earth which spins around on its axis like a top, one turn every day. This movement makes the Sun appear to travel around the Earth. The place where you live points toward the Sun in the day, and away from it at night.

The Earth spins on its axis at a great speed: the surface of the Earth moves at about 1,600km/h (1,000 mph). Gravity provides the force which stops us being thrown off the Earth. Gravity extends a long way from the Earth, and pulls anything within its range toward the Earth. The Moon and artificial satellites are held in orbit around the Earth by the pull of its gravity.

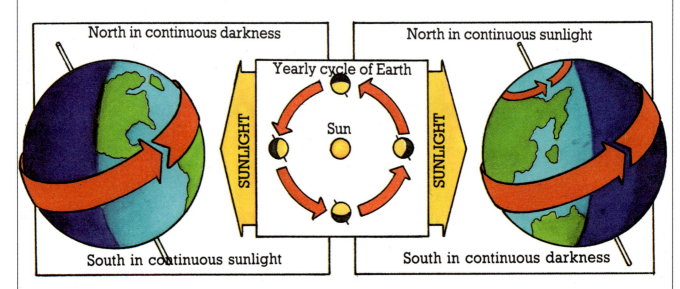

North in continuous darkness

North in continuous sunlight

SUNLIGHT

Yearly cycle of Earth

Sun

SUNLIGHT

South in continuous sunlight

South in continuous darkness

## The seasons

The seasons are caused by the Earth's orbit around the Sun. The diagram shows how the Earth's axis is slanted. During winter in the northern world, the midday Sun is over a region south of the equator, so the rays reaching the north spread out over a larger area. They are less concentrated. During summer the Sun is over a region north of the equator, so its rays are more concentrated and feel hotter. Places south of the equator have their summer when places north of the equator have winter.

The Earth seen from space clearly shows areas of night and day

The hottest and driest climates on Earth are found in the deserts

# CLIMATE

Different areas of the globe have widely ranging types of climate. For example, we expect the climate to be hotter as we travel toward the equator. This is because at the equator the Sun's rays are more concentrated; the diagram below shows how the Sun's rays fall both on the equator and the poles.

Places near the sea are usually cooler in summer, and warmer in winter, than places far from the sea. This is because the sea heats up and cools down less easily than the land, and so keeps the land warm in winter and cool in summer.

These differences in temperature cause movements of air across the Earth's surface, called winds. Air movements, in turn, cause clouds to form, as warm, moist air is cooled by rising up over hills.

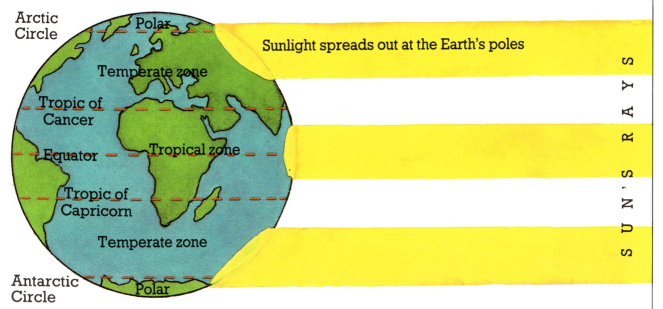

The Sun's rays reaching the Earth near the equator are spread over a smaller area than rays reaching the Earth near the poles. This means that sunlight reaching polar regions is less intense than sunlight reaching the equator. It also means that places near the poles are colder than places near the equator.

# THE ATMOSPHERE

The air you breathe forms a thin layer – the "atmosphere" – around the Earth. It only reaches upward for a few hundred miles. As you go higher, there is less air. Even at the height where planes fly, there would be too little air to breathe.

Most plants and animals need the atmosphere in order to live. The part of the air that you need to breathe is "oxygen," but oxygen is only about a fifth of the air. The rest is mostly "nitrogen." Plants rely on a small amount of "carbon dioxide" in the air to make their food and the food we eat. In addition, the air contains small amounts of other gases, and some water vapor and dust. Between the "stratosphere" and "ionosphere" is an "ozone" layer. Ozone, which is a form of oxygen, prevents harmful ultraviolet rays from the Sun reaching the Earth's surface.

The dramatic aurora lights up the atmosphere

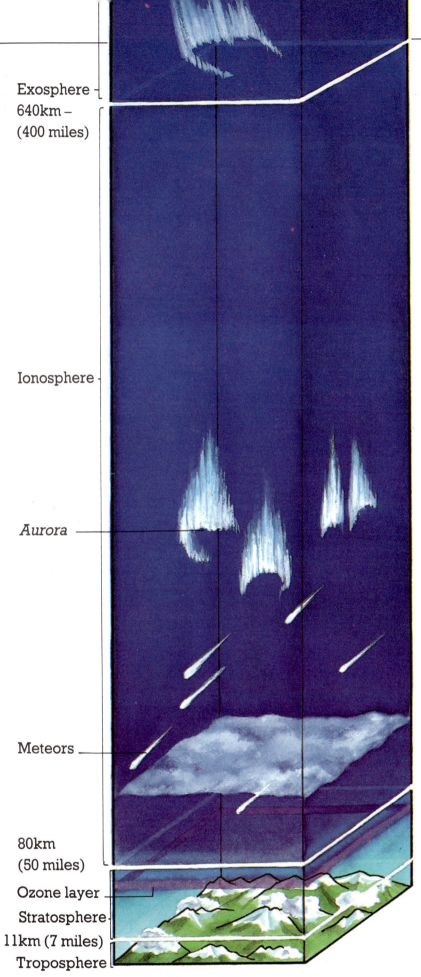

Exosphere
640km –
(400 miles)

Ionosphere

Aurora

Meteors

80km
(50 miles)

Ozone layer

Stratosphere

11km (7 miles)
Troposphere

## Exosphere
The highest, outer region of the Earth's atmosphere is called the "exosphere." Here, conditions are not very different from outer space as there is only very little air indeed.

## Ionosphere
The "ionosphere" is made up of electrically charged particles produced when the Sun's radiation hits the upper atmosphere. Near the poles, this causes a brilliant display of lights, the "aurora."

## Stratosphere
The "stratosphere" extends up to about 80km (50 miles) above Earth. As you travel upward in this layer, the temperature rises slightly, nevertheless temperatures are below freezing point.

## Troposphere
The "troposphere" contains the air we breathe. Clouds, rain and snow all form in this layer. As you travel up through the troposphere, it becomes colder.

25

# EARTH'S BALANCE

The parts of the world affecting our lives are called our "environment." This includes the Earth's crust, oceans, atmosphere, plants and animals. If the balance between things added to the environment and things taken away is upset, then the environment will change.

Many of the things we take from the Earth, like metals and fossil fuels, take millions of years to be replaced naturally, and will run out if we use them up too fast. Other things, like wood from trees, are replaced more quickly, but if we use them too fast, then forests will disappear, to be replaced by other types of landscape. Some things we produce, like poisons and waste, are not removed as quickly as we add them to our environment, so they build up, causing pollution.

Pollution from industry can cause changes in the Earth's atmosphere

Cutting down huge forests can also disturb the Earth's balance

# MAKE YOUR OWN ORRERY

An "orrery" is a model which shows how the planets move in their orbits about the Sun. In this model you can see how the Earth travels around the Sun and how, at the same time, the Moon travels about the Earth. The planets are not made to any realistic scale as the Sun is many thousands of times larger than the Earth.

**What you need**
3 Cocktail sticks
Thin white cardboard
Thumbtack
Clay
Scissors
Compass

1. Draw five circles using a compass, and a square, to the measurements listed below. Cut out the shapes from the cardboard.

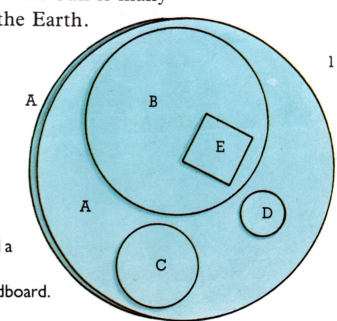

A=3¾ in. (twice) B=2⅜ in. C=⅞ in. D=½ in., (all radii) E=1½×1½ in.

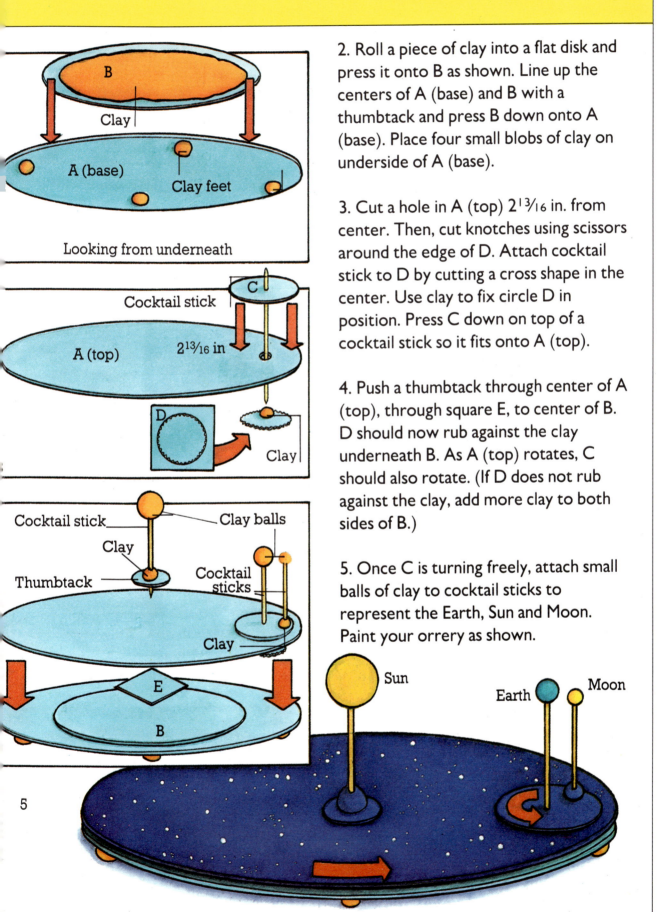

Looking from underneath

Clay

B

A (base)

Clay feet

Cocktail stick

A (top)

2¹³⁄₁₆ in

C

D

Clay

Cocktail stick

Clay balls

Clay

Thumbtack

Cocktail sticks

Clay

E

B

2. Roll a piece of clay into a flat disk and press it onto B as shown. Line up the centers of A (base) and B with a thumbtack and press B down onto A (base). Place four small blobs of clay on underside of A (base).

3. Cut a hole in A (top) 2¹³⁄₁₆ in. from center. Then, cut knotches using scissors around the edge of D. Attach cocktail stick to D by cutting a cross shape in the center. Use clay to fix circle D in position. Press C down on top of a cocktail stick so it fits onto A (top).

4. Push a thumbtack through center of A (top), through square E, to center of B. D should now rub against the clay underneath B. As A (top) rotates, C should also rotate. (If D does not rub against the clay, add more clay to both sides of B.)

5. Once C is turning freely, attach small balls of clay to cocktail sticks to represent the Earth, Sun and Moon. Paint your orrery as shown.

Sun

Earth

Moon

5

## Moving Crust

As the plates of the Earth's surface move toward each other, one plate may rise over the other one. The one which goes up forms mountains, and the one which goes down is slowly melted below the Earth's surface. Where two plates move away from each other, magma is free to escape. It solidifies to form rock, and either a "mid-ocean ridge" or a "volcanic island" is formed.

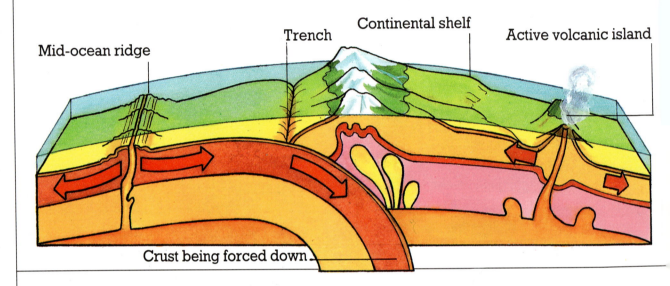

Mid-ocean ridge

Trench

Continental shelf

Active volcanic island

Crust being forced down

## Folding

Movements in the Earth's plates can also cause the Earth's surface to buckle and split. Where the surface splits and slips, a "fault" is produced. Where the surface buckles, a "fold" is formed. Many familiar features of the landscape are caused by folds and faults, and these can often be seen in layers of rocks at seaside cliffs. The diagram shows some of the features that can be produced in these ways.

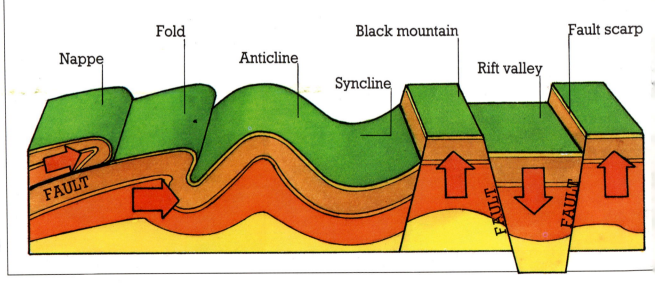

Nappe

Fold

Anticline

Syncline

Black mountain

Rift valley

Fault scarp

FAULT

FAULT

FAULT

# GLOSSARY

**Atmosphere**
The layer of air surrounding the Earth. As you go higher into the atmosphere, the temperature and the nature of the atmosphere change.

**Aurora**
A brilliant display of lights seen in the sky near the North and South Poles, caused by charged particles from the Sun hitting the atmosphere.

**Axis**
An imaginary line which goes from the North Pole to the South Pole, through the middle of the Earth. The Earth spins around this line.

**Continental Drift**
Slow movement of the tectonic plates over millions of years. Originally, the continents were close together; they spread apart as the tectonic plates moved.

**Core**
The central region of the Earth, made up of solid metallic rock surrounded by molten rock.

**Crust**
The solid surface skin of the Earth. It floats on a layer of fluid rock called the mantle.

**Environment**
The parts of the Earth where we live. The environment includes the crust, atmosphere, oceans, plants and animals.

**Gravity**
Everything on the Earth, or nearby, is pulled toward the center of the Earth. This pull is called gravity.

**Ice Age**
A period of time when much of the Earth's surface was covered for thousands of years by a thick layer of ice. During the last ice age, much of Canada and Northern Europe was covered by ice.

**Mantle**
The region of the Earth's interior beneath the crust. Just below the crust, the mantle is molten, but several hundred miles down it becomes more solid.

**Plankton**
Microscopic plants and animals which live in the top few feet of the oceans. They provide food for many sea animals.

**Pollution**
Occurs when humans add things like poisons and rubbish to the environment faster than they can be removed.

**Sediment**
Small particles which settle out as a layer when fast-moving water carrying sand or mud slows down.

**Tectonic Plates**
Large flat plates, thousands of miles across, which make up the surface of the Earth.

# INDEX

**Photographic Credits:**
Cover: Daily Telegraph; title page and pages 6, 10, 13, 15 and 17: Zefa; contents page and pages 7 and 24: Art Directors; page 9: Robert Harding; pages 21, 22 and 27: Tony Stone; page 26: Rex Features.